PIANO · VOCAL · GUITAR

CHART HITS OF '

M000099297

ISBN 0-7935-3188-8

HAL·LEONARD™
CORPORATION

7777 W. BLUEMOUND RD. P.O. BOX 13819 MILWAUKEE, WI 53213

CONTENTS

ALL ABOUT SOUL

Words and Music by
BILLY JOEL

She waits for me ___ at night,
peo - ple who ___ have lost

she waits for me ___ in si - lence.
ev - 'ry trace of hu - man kind - ness. There She are

get - ting out of con - trol _____ should drive her a - way.
in that old rock 'n' roll, _____ but that's on - ly part,

So, why does she stay? It's all a - bout
you know in your heart it's all a - bout

soul. _____
soul. _____

ALL THAT SHE WANTS

Words and Music by JOKER, BUDDHA, LINN and JENNY

She leads a lone - ly _ life. _

She leads a lone - ly _ life. _

Well she woke up late in the morn - ing light and the

14

15

ALL FOR LOVE

(From Walt Disney Pictures' "THE THREE MUSKETEERS")

Words and Music by BRYAN ADAMS,
ROBERT JOHN "MUTT" LANGE and MICHAEL KAMEN

ANOTHER SAD LOVE SONG

Words and Music by BABYFACE
and DARYL SIMMONS

AMAZING

Words and Music by STEVEN TYLER
and RICHIE SUPA

Guitar solo - ad lib.

BED OF ROSES

Words and Music by
JON BON JOVI

Lyrics:
Sit-ting here wast-ed and wound-ed at this old pi-an-o
i-ron-clad fist I wake up and French kiss the morn-ing
so far a-way that each step that I take is on my way home.
try - ing
while some
A king's

37

38

40

BREATHE AGAIN

Words and Music by
BABYFACE

CAN'T HELP FALLING IN LOVE

Words and Music by GEORGE DAVID WEISS,
HUGO PERETTI and LUIGI CREATORE

47

CRYIN'

Words and Music by STEVEN TYLER,
JOE PERRY and TAYLOR RHODES

COME UNDONE

Written by
DURAN DURAN

57

DREAMLOVER

Words and Music by MARIAH CAREY
and DAVE HALL

Do do do do do do do, ooh _____

ba - by. _____

I need a lov - er to give _____ me
I don't want an - oth - er pre - tend - er _____

DON'T WALK AWAY

Words and Music by VASSAL BENFORD
and RON SPEARMAN

MCA music publishing

FIELDS OF GOLD

Words and Music by
STING

73

FOREVER IN LOVE

By KENNY G

(Sax fills - ad lib.)

GOODY GOODY

Words and Music by DURAN RAMOS
and KENNY DIAZ

HAVE I TOLD YOU LATELY

Words and Music by
VAN MORRISON

Slowly, with expression

HERO

Words and Music by MARIAH CAREY
and WALTER AFANASIEFF

and you'll fin - 'ly see ___ the truth ___ that a he - ro lies ___ in you. ___

It's a

Lord knows ___ dreams are hard ___ to fol - low,

but don't let an - y - one ___ tear them a - way. ___ Hold ___ on, ___

HOPELESSLY

Words and Music by RICK ASTLEY
and ROB FISHER

I DON'T WANNA FIGHT

(From The Touchstone Motion Picture "WHAT'S LOVE GOT TO DO WITH IT")

Words and Music by BILLY LAWRIE,
LULU FRIEDA and STEVE DU BERRY

I'D DO ANYTHING FOR LOVE
(BUT I WON'T DO THAT)

Words and Music by
JIM STEINMAN

104

110

IF I EVER FALL IN LOVE

Words and Music by
CARL MARTIN

MCA music publishing

114

IF I EVER LOSE MY FAITH IN YOU

Words and Music by
STING

IN THE STILL OF THE NITE
(I'LL REMEMBER)

Words and Music by
FRED PARRIS

REASON TO BELIEVE

Words and Music by
TIM HARDIN

JESSIE

Words and Music by
JOSHUA KADISON

LINGER

Lyrics by DOLORES O'RIORDAN
Music by DOLORES O'RIORDAN and NOEL HOGAN

LOOKING THROUGH PATIENT EYES

(Contains sample from "Father Figure")

Words and Music by ATTRELL CORDES
and GEORGE MICHAEL

MCA music publishing

148

ORDINARY WORLD

Written by
DURAN DURAN

THE POWER OF LOVE

Words by MARY SUSAN APPLEGATE and JENNIFER RUSH
Music by CANDY DEROUGE and GUNTHER MENDE

RAIN

Words and Music by SHEP PETTIBONE
and MADONNA

RUN TO YOU
(From the film "THE BODYGUARD")

Words and Music by ALLAN RICH
and JUD FRIEDMAN

MCA music publishing

THE RIVER OF DREAMS

Words and Music by
BILLY JOEL

180

WHEN I FALL IN LOVE
(Featured In The TriStar Motion Picture "SLEEPLESS IN SEATTLE")

Words by EDWARD HEYMAN
Music by VICTOR YOUNG

When I fall in love it will be for- ev- er, __ or I'll nev- er fall in love. __

In a rest- less world like this is, __ love is end- ed be- fore it's be-

182

ROCK AND ROLL DREAMS COME THROUGH

Words and Music by
JIM STEINMAN

MCA music publishing

I nev-er want to lose ___ it.
I want to show you how to use ___ it.
You've been through the
You've been through a lot of

fi - res of hell ___ and I know you've got the ash - es to prove ___
pain in the dirt ___ and I know you've got the scars ___ to prove ___

___ it.
___ it.
Re - mem-ber ev-'ry-thing that I told ___

___ you, and I'm tell-ing you a - gain that it's true. ___ When you're a -
You're

SIMPLE LIFE

Words and Music by
ELTON JOHN and BERNIE TAUPIN

TELL ME WHAT YOU DREAM

Words and Music by JOSH LEO,
TIMOTHY B. SCHMIT and VINCE MELAMED

All of your life____ you hold out for love; ___ you
Deep in the night __ you whis-per so low. ___ I

TRUE LOVE

Words and Music by
COLE PORTER

208

TWO PRINCES

Words and Music by
SPIN DOCTORS

213

A WHOLE NEW WORLD
(Aladdin's Theme)
(From Walt Disney's "Aladdin")

Music by ALAN MENKEN
Lyrics by TIM RICE

Moderately, sweetly

Male: I can show you the world, I can o-pen your eyes

shin - ing, shim - mer - ing, splen - did. Tell me, prin - cess, now
take you won - der by won - der o - ver, side - ways and

when did you last let your heart de - cide?
un - der on a

220